Top Dog

a managerial satire

by

Clark Crouch

Top Dog

a managerial satire

by
Clark Crouch

Being a segment of my life wherein I learn the continuing value of the traditional functions of management and lose my employment. The foibles of Rascals and Tramps are exposed, together with the processes by which management training programs are repackaged to meet the fads of the day. I begin a new career.

Copyright ©1993, 2014 by Clark Crouch.
All rights reserved including the right of reproduction in whole or in part in any form. First published in a limited edition by *The Resource Network,* April 1993.

ISBN-13: 978-1505728347
ISBN-10: 1505728347

The Resource Network
Woodinville, Washington

Contents

Contents v

Preface vi

Acknowledgments viii

My Diary 1

Planning 7

Organizing 9

Staffing 12

Leading 15

Controlling 18

Author 23

Books authored/edited by Clark Crouch

Voices of the Wind (free verse)
Reflections (free verse)
Where Horses Reign
Sun, Sand & Soapweed
Western Images
Views from the Saddle
Eight Viewpoints (8 poet anthology)
Harkin' Home
Thirty
Rustic Ruminations*
Western Viewpoints (16 poet anthology)
Poetic Reflectons At The Creekside (30 poet anthology)
Prairie Knights
Ridin' & Writin' (Vol. 1)**
Ridin' & Writing' (Vol.2***

* Reprint of *Voices of the Wind* and *Reflections*
** Reprint of *Where Horses Reign* and *Sun, Sand & Soapweed*
*** Reprint of *Western Images* and *Views from the Saddle*

Preface

In this time of quick fixes, this book has cried out to be written. The fundamentals of management have been packaged and repackaged to fit the buzz words of the times. Attempts have been made to create "sciences" of trivia which are, at best, just tools for the manager to use in accomplishing the task of management.

Tools are important, even vital--tools such as assessments, statistical quality control, self-managing work teams, empowerment, and participative management do facilitate and ease the manager's role-- but they remain subordinate to the basic functions of management.

New tools may be needed at times to accommodate the unique needs of people. However, the basic functions of management do not change as a result of the manager's sex or sexual persuasion, race, religion, politics, or occupation. Neither do the essential functions of management change as the result of any difference or diversity among those in the workplace. The demand is for managers to manage and to treat each person as an individual with sensitivity, equality, honesty, and fairness.

This slender book has but one premise--managers can survive, be successful, and achieve quality, excellence, and productivity, if they know and practice the basics of management--planning, organizing, staffing, leading, and controlling!

As Ross Perot, a presidential candidate in 1992, might have said, "It's that simple. Let's get on with it!"

Acknowledgments

A great many people have influenced and shaped my life and this book. Over the past sixty-eight years, I have met many and worked with many outstanding individuals who have stuck to the fundamentals despite the pressure to offer quick fixes. Several have made a very special impression:

- Kenneth Blanchard and Paul Hersey, who together gave a new meaning to "leadership"

- W. Edwards Deming, who enriched industry through statistical quality control processes

- Peter F. Drucker, who advocated the basics to address the challenges of today and tomorrow

- R. Alec Mackenzie, who figuratively saved managers two hours a day via time management

- David W. Merrill, who enhanced our understanding of the social needs of individuals

- Ronald Reagan who demonstrated the courage of his convictions in local and national offices

- Helen Reynolds, who advocated a down-home, pragmatic approach to using the basics

- Ralph C. Smedley, who founded Toastmasters International and gave managers a voice

- Harry Truman who did not shy away from some the most difficult decisions of the 20th Century

My Diary

July 1

Today I was fired from Rascals and Tramps (RAT), the nation's top management training firm. I don't know why, really. All I said was they were trying to repackage the same old stuff under today's buzz words. Maybe I did get a bit carried away; perhaps I shouldn't have called it the big lie! In any case, I'm job hunting again.

On the way home, I bought some fancy bond paper for my resume. Should I use the traditional white or use an astro color to get attention? So many decisions.

July 2

Looking back five years, I had just received a master's degree in organizational development. Almost immediately I was accepted at Rascals and Tramps to work on a program for the Midwest Medical Foundation.

The foundation's management was caught up in the Deming approach to quality control and wanted it adapted to the medical field. All well and good! Dr. Deming, in addition to his innovative statistical quality control processes, emphasizes good, traditional management--planning, organizing, staffing, leading, and controlling. The future looked pretty bright.

Then I started work on the project. All was not well and good.

RAT management pulled a 1970 version of a basic management training program off the shelf. We changed "management" to "total quality management" (TQM) throughout the text, prepared a new cover with the foundation's logo and a caduceus, and sent a consultant out to teach the "new" technology!

Meanwhile, another version (without the logo) was prepared and advertised nationally as the definitive, state-of-the-art TQM program for the health care field.

Other covers, these without the caduceus, were prepared: *TQM for Manufacturing, TQM for Nonprofits,* etc. It was the beginning of RAT's climb to the top of the training heap.

My next task assignment was similar. A manufacturing company wanted a program on SMWT (self-managed work teams). Not to worry. Off the shelf we again pulled the basic management training program, changed "manager" to "team leader" throughout, designed a custom cover, and sent forth another RAT emissary.

Naturally, a commercial version was prepared and successfully promoted. RAT was on the cutting edge of training technology!

Under a contract with the State Office of Women's Business Enterprises to develop a management training program for women, we went through the basic management program for a third time. We changed "he" to "she", changed the title to *Women as Managers,* and again had a best selling program with consultants on the road throughout the United States. Top drawer stuff; we were really out in front of the competition!

During the five years, we really honed the cutting edge, pounding that basic program into plowshares with such labels as: *Managing for Excellence, Managing for Quality, Managing for Productivity, Situational Management, Grid Management, Managing Customer Service, Managing Time, Managing Transformation, Participative Management, Managing Diversity,* and *Managing by Matrix.* RAT became the leader of the pack.

I don't know exactly when I began to develop a professional conscience. Somewhere during the process of selling that tired old program about twenty times under different names, I realized what we were really doing. Then, yesterday, I made the "big lie" comment and got sacked.

Tomorrow I start looking toward a new career.

July 3

Spent the day revising my resume.

One thing about it, my experience at RAT really taught me how to tailor a document to target the market. I now have twelve versions of the resume and fifteen versions of a transmittal letter. Ready for any situation!

I also called my mentor, Professor James Kidwell at my graduate school, to let him know I was available and why.

July 6

After all that work, I may not get to use my resume after all.

Professor Kidwell called this morning and has set up an appointment for me to see Henry Coswell, the chairman of the board for one of the largest department store chains in the United States, CosMart.

Kidwell says that Coswell is the greatest trainer in the world. We'll see. My appointment is for tomorrow.

July 7

How do I begin? This has been the strangest day of my life. First, I did keep my appointment with Henry Coswell. Apparently my professor had already told him much about me because the interview really didn't last very long. He didn't even inquire as to why I had left RAT. In fact, he seemed more interested in talking about the philosophy of management than anything else.

I specifically remember one comment he made, "Son, there is no mystery in being a good manager. Anyone who can plan, organize, staff, lead, and control can get quality, productivity, excellence, and all the rest."

At one point, I remember asking about the need for real management programs to meet today's needs in things like diversity in the workplace, women as managers, and participative management.

He answered with a question, "So, what's different?" Then he went on to explain that a manager is a manager and the skills that are needed are the same regardless of diversity, or sex, or employee involvement. "Don't complicate it, son, there is no difference."

The meeting was over in half an hour. As I was leaving, Mr. Coswell asked that I come back tomorrow. "I'd like to match the salary you were getting with Rascals and Tramps and put you on a special management training program. Think about it and we'll talk."

What a day! And what a shame about all the resumes-- astro-cherry paper is quite striking.

July 8

Yesterday was strange?

This morning I met again with Henry Coswell. I accepted his offer. No sooner had I said yes than Mr. Coswell snapped his fingers. Out from behind the lounge in the corner of the room came the biggest black Labrador I had ever seen.

"This is Trainer," he said. "Trainer will be your companion and instructor throughout your program. You will have no duties except to care for Trainer and meet with me once a week to review your progress. Any questions?"

I should have had questions! I know I should have, but I was so speechless as Mr. Coswell snapped a leash on Trainer and handed it over to me. "I'll see you a week from today, same time. Good luck, my boy!"

July 11

I have not had time to write for several days. Old dog Trainer is certainly demanding. First, shopping for food--he seems to prefer human food--then a stop at a pet store for other stuff. I begin to wonder about all the things they said I would need --brush, flea powder, bed, blanket, jacket, tooth powder and brush, ear oil, vitamins, nail clippers and file, and more!

I take comfort in knowing I have the tools to keep Trainer groomed and healthy. I hardly feel that the comfort I feel is worth the $397.42 of canine equipage that takes up my entire kitchen counter.

July 14

Kept my appointment with Mr. Coswell. Spent about thirty minutes talking about how Trainer and I were getting adjusted. I mentioned the $397.42 in passing but Mr. Coswell did not grab at the possibly too subtle hint to reimburse me.

Planning

Establishing goals and objectives, determining a course of action to achieve them, identifying the resources needed, and assigning responsibility for their accomplishment.

July 15

The word for today is Planning. I define it as determining a course of action, identifying the resources needed to achieve a goal or objective, and assigning responsibility.

I had thought at first that old Trainer was napping and inattentive to things going on around him. Now I realize the depth of his thinking. Not the slightest thing seems to escape his attention, especially if it is something that might bug me.

Take this morning, for example. I had hardly gotten out of bed and getting ready to shower until Trainer was pacing up and down the hall between the bathroom and the back door with a whine on his lips and a strange look in his eye. I should not have gone ahead with the shower.

By the time I got to the kitchen to get my first cup of coffee for the day. Trainer was lying down peacefully on the sofa. His eyes were closed, the only sound was that of his thoughtful breathing, and my professional journals were soaked. Why didn't he say he needed to go out? Why is he planning against me?

I immediately grabbed him by the collar, marched him to the door, and shoved him out into the yard. This too must have been part of his plan. After he had been out for some thirty minutes and I had finished my third cup of coffee, I went to the back door only to discover the rest of Trainer's plot.

There he lay in the midst of my prize herb garden--plants dug up and strewn around to expose the cool bare earth where he lay, eyes closed, planning ever new strategies to plague me.

Just a few minutes ago, Trainer came sauntering into my study, whined at me, and walked out toward the living room. He led me to my stack of journals, freshly soaked, then to the back door to be let out. I know he's out there now, lying in cool luxury, planning how he will manage my life.

July 21

Met again with Mr. Coswell. He seems more interested in what Trainer and I are doing than in my management training. A thought crosses my mind--what have I gotten myself into? A most unusual situation. He did smile at my description of Trainer's planning process.

Organizing

Bringing together the resources needed to accomplish goals and objectives. Resources are people, property, time, money, and technology (knowledge).

July 25

The word for today is Organizing. In my mind, organizing means marshaling the necessary resources and using them to accomplish a goal or objective. Trainer seems to have developed those resources and, I guess from his perspective, he does use them effectively. His ultimate goal escapes me.

Yesterday was a disaster. Old Trainer appears to have finally finished with the planning phase of whatever operation he has in mind. He is now into the implementation phase--really beginning to get things organized, especially in the back yard.

Trainer has set aside the Southeast corner of the yard as the most appropriate spot to erect monuments commemorating whatever Labradors commemorate.

He apparently did not consider that my salad garden was there first. My prize lettuce has disappeared and the garden is now a place that one would scarcely want to walk let alone to harvest anything for the table.

Trainer has also reorganized a significant section of the lawn next to my obnoxious neighbor's fence. My neighbor, Sam Smythe (I think he spells it that way just to be uppity!), has a little Cocker Spaniel in perpetual heat.

Trainer, not apparently realizing what a little bitch she is, has been parading across the lawn stiff legged, scratching tremendous divots into the air just to impress her.

Then there is the matter of the garbage can. Half of it is gone, together with the lid, its contents are more-or-less organized through the back yard, and a portion of the contents appears to have become bedding in my reorganized herb garden.

Much later in the day. Trainer has been walking the back yard with a pleased look on his jowls and has erected a new monument to commemorate his latest accomplishments. I may have located the major portion of the garbage can. With no suitable repository available to collect all the stuff, I seem to be at Trainer's mercy. I must get a new can very soon.

Much, much later. The planning phase may not be quite completed. Trainer has discovered that the back fence is no barrier to his paternal instinct to organize a family. I fail to understand Sam Smythe's irritation in the matter--waving his hoe and shouting untranslatable things at Trainer, and at me as well.

Trainer has now begun to eye the front yard--a fertile field for exercising his organizational talents. Obviously, the fence will be no barrier for Trainer.

I plan to go to the store for fresh lettuce for dinner although I admit that I may just have soup this evening and forego any salad.

July 28

My weekly meeting with Mr. Coswell. A most unusual gentleman. We did talk a bit about organizing as a function of a good manager. I rather think he takes a perverse pleasure in hearing of the difficulties I have had in the past several weeks.

I regret that we did not speak further and more directly of management. However, the meeting was short as Mr. Coswell seemed somewhat preoccupied.

Staffing

Selecting, hiring, training, and coordinating human resources and assuring that they have the necessary responsibilities, authorities, and resources to attain goals and objectives.

August 3

The word for today is Staffing. Mr. Coswell reminded me in our last conversation that this is organizing the people part of achieving goals. Work goes more easily when the right people are involved.

Mr. Coswell also confirmed my belief that it is easier to find and hire the right person that it is to fire a wrong one. Unfortunately, I had no voice in Trainer's selection and, in any case, I cannot fire him.

I have decided, however, to use a bit of psychology and some participatory management techniques to get Trainer to accept more ownership and responsibility for the way things look around here.

A friend of many years ago, Dr. Smedley, once said, "People learn best in moments of enjoyment." That may be just the clue I need to get Trainer productively involved. Even though he is not a "people" he might respond.

Something certainly needs to be done. The first thing this morning Sam Smythe was at it again--yelling and shouting and being generally obnoxious--just because Trainer had made a nocturnal visit to his back yard and dug up five rose bushes. I suspect our occasional friendship may be ending on a sour note. I do admit a temptation to shout back or to call the police about the way he is disturbing the peace--just let him take one step into my yard, preferably into the salad garden.

Later in the day I found my old ball and glove in the attic. What pleasant memories.

Trainer and I played ball--toss and fetch--trying to learn in moments of enjoyment. Actually, he is not terribly bright. I would toss the ball and he would lie watching it with great interest. I would then fetch the ball and take it to him. He would mouth it and toss it into the air until exhaustion demanded that he lie down again.

We would then repeat the process. We had fun until I realized two things: first, while I was fetching, Trainer had chewed up my ball glove; and, second, Trainer was getting me to do all of the work. Stupid dog! I have returned the ball and glove (the latter in a little bag to keep the pieces together) to the attic.

We do seem to be getting along quite well. Sam is keeping his Spaniel inside his house somewhere, Trainer has not yet leaped the fence to claim my front yard, we have a new garbage can (one that holds 105 gallons), Trainer has not yet discovered where I have hidden my professional journals, and we purchase our salad greens from the grocer.

August 4

Visited Mr. Coswell. We discussed advertising and marketing. I never did understand the difference, but refrained from saying so.

August 11

Trainer accompanied me to see Mr. Coswell today.

Last week while I was gone, Trainer found my collection of professional journals in a cabinet I had accidentally left open. Those that were not newly wetted were torn apart and had been used to create a nest beside the fancy bed I had bought for him.

When I arrived home, he seemed rather pleased with his accomplishments, bounding around the house, smiling in his own way as he led me to view his handiwork. Obviously, planning and organizing are a continuing process with Trainer.

Mr. Coswell seemed pleased to see Trainer, just as Trainer was pleased to see him. There was a grand inspection of Trainer's teeth, his ears, his paws. There were nods of approval from Mr. Coswell and several self-satisfied smiles and tail wags from Trainer. That accomplished, we talked a bit about the upcoming elections.

What has all this to do with management?

Leading

Assuring that the right people do the right things, the right way, at the right time, at the most effective use of resources--creating an environment that helps people become motivated participants. It involves inspiring, rewarding, disciplining, and communicating.

August 12

The word for today is Leading. In today's workplace the process of leadership can involve self-directed teams, employee participation, and all that. Still, basically, Mr. Coswell says it's getting the right people to do the right things, the right way, at the right time. In the old days, this was called "directing" and I am tempted occasionally to revert to those authoritarian times in order to redirect Trainer's efforts.

To exercise my leadership, I have given in and enrolled Trainer and myself in a pet training class. He has a much easier time than I, undoubtedly he has been through the class several times before. I find the burden of leadership to be such a chore. However, I have been using Trainer's leash more frequently and find that it helps to guide him more or less in the direction I want him to go--unless he happens to use his 90 pounds to leverage me into going his direction.

All has gone well in the class except for the cat incident. I will not write of it except to say that it was not my fault, nor that of Trainer. What business does a cat have ripping through a dog training class anyhow?

My attorney says I should pay for Mrs. Donnelson's wig but I do feel it looked much like the cat and Trainer was just reacting naturally. The law should recognize that cats and dogs are not friendly. Otherwise, why should they fight like cats and dogs? After all, it was Mrs. Donnelson who brought the cat there in the first place! I shall stand on principle!

Later in the day. Good news. Sam Smythe has moved. This morning a truck was in front of his place. By noon it was loaded and gone and Sam, with Spaniel, followed it away in his station wagon. Perhaps we shall have neighbors that are a bit friendlier and less inclined to shout so much.

I've just gone to answer the door only to have a summons stuck into my hand by a scroungy looking individual. Sam has elected to sue me. It seems that his Spaniel, which he now claims to be a purebred, is pregnant, presumably by Trainer. The thing also cites five rose bushes, a dozen tomato plants, and a score of other items which trainer is said to have destroyed or reorganized.

August 18

Unable to meet with Mr. Coswell. He was most understanding that it was important for me to keep a court appointment. If only the judge had been equally understanding--$932 paid to Sam Smythe.

What is the world coming to when a bitchy little Spaniel is allowed to be kept in a fine residential neighborhood and to entice law-abiding pets like Trainer into transgressing?

I am happy that Smythe has gone and good riddance even at the price I've had to pay. Since I've paid for them, I've taken all the ripe tomatoes from those plants which survived Trainer's alleged attack. I shall enjoy every bite knowing that loudmouth Smythe is gone.

August 19

My birthday! Although it is mid-week, Trainer and I took the day off and wandered around in the park. Not too long after we arrived, Trainer spotted Mrs. Donnelson walking her cat. I could scarcely contain him as he began dancing about trying to get at the little beast.

Mrs. Donnelson jousted him with her umbrella and threatened to call the police. Pulling Trainer along, I left the park hurriedly.

We spent the rest of the day watching the antics of the gulls at the city land fill. I scarcely believe Mrs. Donnelson will take her cat out there even though it would be an appropriate repository for those horrible wigs she wears.

Controlling

Regulating and evaluating the work in progress. It involves establishing, implementing, and monitoring policies, procedures, and schedules for performance, inspection, reporting, and feedback.

August 20

The word for today is Controlling. This management function involves making sure that things happen appropriately by coordinating, checking, cross-checking, reporting, etc.

At first, the only way I seemed to be able to control Trainer was by keeping him on a leash. Recently, however, I have established clear-cut parameters and controls for his conduct and have insisted that he observe them.

A pet door has been installed so Trainer can go in and out as his body urges; the new garbage can has been chained to the wall of the house; the back fence has been extended to six feet in height; the salad garden has been spaded under; and Trainer has the full run of the back yard, including the herb garden. He seems especially fond of catnip. Strange creature but as soon as I had the controls in place he became a model of decorum.

Someone is already moving into the Smythe house--I'm tempted to write his name as "Smith" just to show him what for. Whoever it is shall certainly be better than Smythe. At very least, we shall start off on a more friendly, neighborly basis. I celebrate Smythe's departure.

August 25

Met with Mr. Coswell for an extended period. We reviewed all of the events since I entered the management training program on July the 8th. Then Mr. Coswell made a little speech which I place in quotes below even though it may not be quite verbatim.

"My boy, you've come through with flying colors. From our conversations I can tell that Trainer has performed well in teaching you the management skills you will need to work for CosMart. You've gained knowledge and practical experience in planning, organizing, staffing, leading, and controlling.

"Knowing these basic functions of management, you will be able to achieve quality and productivity while leading your people in a fair and participative way. You don't need the fancy buzz words and acronyms to be a successful manager in a successful organization--just good management sense."

With all that said, he presented me a fine, engraved certificate, a check for my wages to date, a second check in the amount of $1,329.42 in payment of Smythe's court award and Trainer's expenses, and a paper transferring ownership of Trainer to me. I had hardly wished for the latter; however, my home is so well organized to meet his needs that I may come to enjoy his company.

August 27

I feel rather pleased with myself, having done so well as a management trainee, and I look forward to whatever new challenges Mr. Coswell and Trainer place before me.

Later. Trainer has just come inside carrying a ragged hank of hair. Seems to look rather like a cat. Strange!

Still later. Some time ago, Trainer (smiling, I swear) brought in another blob of hair. As he plopped it at my feet, obviously and greatly pleased with himself, I heard shouting from the back. Peeking out, I saw, of all people, Mrs. Donnelson jumping and screaming much worse than Smythe had ever done. And her language! Such a row over such a trifle!

It seems Trainer had climbed the fence, chased the Donnelson cat to the roof of the house, and chewed Mrs. Donnelson's wigs which were out to air, completely destroying the blue one and bringing two of the horrible things back home with him.

Yes, Mrs. Donnelson is our new neighbor, living now in Sam Smythe's house! In retrospect, I am beginning to feel that Smythe may not have really been all that bad.

September 1

My training period ended, I have been named as the Manager of Training and Development for Henry Coswell's CosMart chain. The training instilled and reinforced in me the essential principles of management--planning, organizing, staffing, leading, and controlling--while cautioning that fads are fads and one minute does not make a manager, unless of course it is coupled with a lot of other minutes!

We have a new group of three potential store managers coming in next week for our management training program. In selecting them, I've had each do a personality profile--a doggone good one, if I do say so myself.

Based on the profiles of the new managers, my training staff has its assignments--Trainer Dalmatian will be assigned to Susan of Sioux Falls, Trainer French Poodle will become the mentor of Daniel "Big Dan" of Las Vegas, and Trainer St. Bernard is to work with little Linda Sue of Atlanta.

September 8

Trainer? We are settling into our new lifestyle. He continues as my mentor and advisor but working now on advanced management strategies, corporate acquisitions, etc. Mr. Coswell says he has great expectations of our team and looks forward to moving me upward as fast as Trainer can impart the necessary knowledge and skills.

September 18

Mr. Coswell is talking of leadership training for me. He says the result of good leadership is measured by the three E's...effective, efficient, and economical...that is, suitable for the intended purpose, capable of producing the desired results, and involving the least investment of resources.!

The difference," he says, "between being a manager and being a leader is that a manager goes by the book while the leader writes the book." I should think that is rather an easy way to advance.

Perhaps, one day I shall write a book and thereby become a leader. That would certainly give me a leg up on Trainer!

Author

Clark Crouch has had a varied career – thirty-two years as an administrator for the U.S. Atomic Energy Commission and it's successor organizations, twenty-five years as a management consultant serving an international clientele, and now in retirement, twelve years as a cowboy poet.

He has advised and consulted with scores of governmental, educational, industrial, business and nonprofit organizations throughout the world, facilitating processes such as strategic planning, quality assurance, communications, management, supervision, time management, customer based sales, and related areas.

Specifically in strategic planning, Crouch developed a simplified planning model which is now in use worldwide. It is also taught by several colleges and universities as a part of MBA and other advanced degree programs.

An internationally recognized authority on strategic planning, the author is quoted extensively in professional and academic literature as well as on the internet:

- Strategic Planning is a process by which we can envision the future and develop the necessary procedures and operations to influence and achieve that future.

- No organization's future is predetermined. That future is influenced by a great many constraints, some of which…policies, procedures, economics, competition, laws, regulations, and public opinion…may be mediated, modified, or eliminated by direct and active involvement

- The result of planning should be effective, efficient, and economical…that is, suitable for the intended purpose, capable of producing the desired results, and involving the least investment of resources.

- If it ain't broke, break it, then fix it. Otherwise you may be destined to address tomorrow's problems with yesterday's solutions.

- If you don't know where you're going, you'll probably wind up no where!

- Leadership is getting the right people to do the right thing for the right reason in the right way at the right time at the right use of resources.

- The proper and ethical task of a strategic planning consultant is to build client independence, not dependence on the consultant!

- To be an effective facilitator, you need to enable others to lead the group in the direction they need to go.